Mumtastic!

With love to marvellous mums everywhere

Martha Valentine

PORTICO

With special thanks to Malcolm Croft, Jack Noel, Katie Cowan, Zoe Anspach and all at Anova Books

First published in the United Kingdom in 2010 by
Portico Books
10 Southcombe Street
London
W14 0RA

An imprint of Anova Books Company Ltd

Cover and inside illustrations by Jack Noel (www.jacknoel.co.uk)

ISBN 9781906032616

A CIP catalogue record for this book is available from the British Library.

10 9 8 7 6 5 4 3 2 1

Printed and bound by J.P.Printers SDN. BHD., Malaysia

This book can be ordered direct from the publisher at www.anovabooks.com

For Mum

Introduction

Mums. Aren't they great? They come in all shapes, sizes, varieties and different-coloured packaging. Mums, in fact, are just like the assorted chocolate boxes that Forrest Gump's mum was famous for because, as she put it, 'you never know what you're gonna get'. Indeed, some mums are soft, some are nutty, some smell of liqueur, some are much more fanciable than the others and some even have the potential to break your jaw. No one likes those ones.

It is often argued by scientists there are only two types of mum in the world. The overprotective type of mum who barks 'come down at once' to a child in a tree and the proud type of mum who shouts encouragement to see how much higher they can climb. The wonderful reality is that there are many, many various types of mum, all unique and wonderful in their own little ways – and all mental, scheming and devious in others. This book is a wonderful celebration of them all. Each and every single one.

In a recent survey it was claimed that there are as many species of mum as there are bats, in fact. And, just so you know, that's close to 1000. They may all look the same – hairy, scary and deaf as a post (and that's just the mums) – but most of them are completely different once you stop and appreciate their splendid diversity.

Being a mum means long hours and hard work with no recognition or appreciation. But despite all this, they still turn up for work every day. On time. And with little-to-no fuss. For those reasons alone, they all deserve celebrating. Even though everyone has one, mums are the only creature on planet Earth that is truly, individually, unique.

Though try telling that to a bat.

The only question remains is: *What kind of mum are you?*

Proud-to-be-a-mum Mum

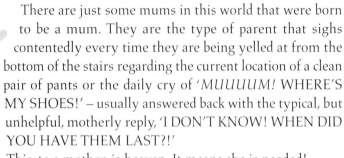

There are just some mums in this world that were born to be a mum. They are the type of parent that sighs contentedly every time they are being yelled at from the bottom of the stairs regarding the current location of a clean pair of pants or the daily cry of '*MUUUUM!* WHERE'S MY SHOES!' – usually answered back with the typical, but unhelpful, motherly reply, 'I DON'T KNOW! WHEN DID YOU HAVE THEM LAST?!'

This, to a mother, is heaven. It means she is needed!

The proud-to-be-a-mum mum uses motherhood to define herself; it's what makes her the happiest, not just in actually being a mum, and loving unconditionally, but in doing the everyday household family chores and tasks with a sense of pizzazz and magic usually reserved for a battle with Voldemort. A proud mum knows that keeping a happy, content home is what keeps a chaotic household running smoothly. This type of mum takes pleasure in knowing she is the big cog that makes the whole family work together and secretly loves the fact that if she wasn't there, then everything would grind screechingly to a halt.

A proud-to-be-a-mum mum is usually seen eagerly at the school gates twenty minutes earlier than any other mum, waiting to ask them how their day was. The usual shrug of 'Yeah, it was alright' will be over-enthusiastically received and welcomed by a mum more than happy to dish out the tightest of hugs, especially after having been deprived for the whole day.

Flirty-with-their-friends Mum

Whether mum flirts in a friendly way – or just because it's fun to embarrass her teenage daughter's new boyfriend or teenage son's male friends – everyone will know a flirty mum. Maybe you are the flirty mum? Oh my, are you blushing? Shame on you!

A flirty-with-their-friends mum usually rushes to the door when their teenage child brings their friends round – much to the embarrassment of said teenager – and begins to act, well, how shall we put it, *very* nicely. A flirty mum may describe her daughter's new boyfriend as 'dishy' or 'dreamy' to her own friends, usually in the sentence

'Jenny brought home her new boyfriend the other day – he's very dreamy, I can see why she likes him – he reminds me of my Paul when he was a young man!'

Maybe you are the type of mum who coos when your teenage son's friends pop round the house because one of them looks a bit like Michael Bublé. 'He's going to be a heartbreaker,' you think to yourself as you swoon and your son dies with mortification in the corner. Either way, your flirtation is nothing more than a bit of fun and the look on your son's face, the embarrassment of having an over-friendly and fun mum, is priceless! Quick, get the camera out!

Have you seen this Mum?

A flirty mum would never call herself a flirty mum, she always uses the excuse that it's 'important to get to know the children's friends, so that they always feel comfortable bringing them round'. Yeah right, whatever, mum!

Naggy-but-in-a-nice-way Mum

Kids! They never learn. Whether it's the toilet seat left up or a bundle of smelly, mud-encrusted football boots left in the hallway or Girls Aloud pumping through the bedroom walls at 10pm on a school night, kids will be kids, and though you love them like crazy, you do wish that, just for once, they would do exactly what you say when you ask them. Or, heavens above, before you have to ask them!

A naggy-but-in-a-nice-way mum hates to nag – she doesn't like being the party pooper or stopping the kids from doing what they enjoy or, even worse, provoking a 'You don't get it!' response from the kids. But when enough is enough, mums have to put the foot down. This type of mum doesn't like to shout, she doesn't like to moan, she likes to make her point and then close the door quietly behind her, hoping that her children understood the seriousness of her tone, but also the gentleness in her voice, and hoping that it will effectively resolve the situation. It rarely works, which is why this type of mum sends dad bounding heavily up the stairs to sort them out. Dad is always more than happy to start shouting because, at the end of the day, his fuse is a lot shorter than mums and he is prepared to put up with a lot less fuss, noise and misbehaviour. Especially if golf is on the telly.

Have you seen this Mum?

Three sentences a mum uses a dozen times a day:
1) 'Tidy your room!'
2) 'Don't use language like that in my house!'
3) 'Take your shoes off please...this isn't a hotel!'

Home-by-11pm Mum (or I'll send your father out looking for you!)

Ah, curfews! Always too early, never quite late enough. And the teenage children will always want more time no matter how relaxed or lenient you have been about it – they'll always stretch you for as far as you will go.

'Be home by 10pm, or I'll send your father out to look for you!' a home-by-11pm mum will say, ready for negotiation.

'Ahhh, mum, make it 11pm – and then I'll definitely be home on time' they'll say thinking that makes sense.

'10.30,' you'll reply, quickly.

'But Jenny's mum lets her stay out until midnight,' the daughter will moan.

'Yes, but that's because Jenny's mum's a....OK, 11pm – but any later and I'll drag your father out of bed to come and look for you.'

Poor dad. He had nothing to do with this, yet it'll be him forced to go out later, just in his slippers and house trousers, driving around the streets making sure their firstborn son is 'not face down in a bush somewhere'. A home-by-11pm mum will panic even more if her child texts them at 10.30pm saying they'll be home in half an hour and then is not walking through the door at precisely 11pm. Of course, how do most kids repay a home-by-11pm mum's very generous curfew time? They stroll in, rebelliously, at 11.05pm, the cheeky so and so's!

Still-wiping-food-off-their-faces Mum

There are some mums who know when to stop. There are some mums who realise that they can't baby their children all their lives (though they'll try) especially when they have flown the nest. And then there are some mums who are completely oblivious to this fact. These are the mums who – no matter how public, uncomfortable or embarrassing it will seem – will lick their thumbs, then wipe smudges, stains or food debris from their children's face much to their annoyance. And it doesn't matter how old they are.

Of course, no wife or husband would ever have the audacity to do that – but mums, well, they are a law unto themselves when it comes to these matters! The mum in question will not understand that she is no longer responsible for her child's cleanliness/appearance any more – no matter how unshaven, dirty or ruffled they may wish to appear. A child's appearance to a mum, at any time, is the most important thing, especially at family social events.

This type of mum likes to think that it doesn't matter how far their children move away, who they marry, what they do in life or how much they protest at being mothered ('aaaah, mum, leave it out'), if a bit of bolognese sauce goes unwiped after a meal – then it's only fair that mum has dibs on cleaning it off first!

Have you seen this Mum?

These mums are a perfect example of the type who always see their son or daughter as 'their baby', regardless of the fact that they are a 31-year-old law graduate who lives with their fiancé!

Texts-the-kids-all-the-time Mum

In this modern world of modern technology mums are having a field day! No longer will mums not know where, or what, their children are getting up to. Mums now have instant access to their kids 24hrs a day, and can find out whether they are loitering at the local shopping mall on a Saturday afternoon, or claiming to be at school when really they are trying to get served at a pub. A mum can now sigh a big sigh of relief, because she can just text them to find out. And if the child has lied about their whereabouts then she has written proof! Texting is less embarrassing (for you) than calling them directly and not quite as devious as calling around other mother's houses to see where they are – just like you would have done before mobile phones came along.

Nowadays, mums who aren't scared of mobile phones are likely to be texting their wandering children at least ten times a day with dubious messages, blatantly trying to pin-point their location and desperately disguising it to make it seem like they are not:

HI, IT'S MUM. I'M GOING OUT NOW BUT WILL BE BACK LATER.
THOUGHT I'D LET YOU KNOW.
WHERE ARE YOU? LOVE MUM XXX

So, while children of this generation may love their mobile phones they will loathe mum texting them all the time to just 'check in' with them. But despite that minor detail, modern mums who know how to use their mobile phones are never more than a (missed) call away from their children.

Makes-a-good-impression Mum

Teenage children bringing their first, or new, boyfriend or girlfriend home to 'meet the parents' is a difficult, embarrassing and, frequently, traumatic experience – especially if you are the type of mum who tries to makes it an even more difficult, embarrassing and traumatic experience by going over the top. Some mums look upon new partners of their grown-up children with suspicion, either measuring them up to the old one (never a good idea!) or making sure they are good enough for their child by evaluating their pros ('ooh, I do like her dress') and cons ('eugh, I don't like her dress') in their head, or by making wild assumptions on their character.

A mum who likes to make a good impression will usually fret about making the house tidy beforehand, plead with dad to put on a non-grubby shirt and (at least) some trousers and also panic over what to cook for dinner. If she is a really nice mum, she'll find out what the girlfriend/boyfriend's favourite type of meal is and cook it much to their pleasant surprise. What a nice touch!

Nothing is more special to a grown-up child than to know their mum agrees with his/her choice of companion. Nothing is more special to a mum than to go *completely* over the top to make them know that she does! Oh, and feel free to bring them home any time, dear!

Wishes-they-were-little-again Mum

When all your children have flown the nest, or when they are behaving particularly rotten towards you for no reason whatsoever, chances are you will drift off happily into dreamland and remember back to the distant past when all your children were only capable of saying two words ('mummy' and 'engine') and all they ever, ever wanted was to never leave your side, grabbing tightly to your legs as if it was the safest place in the world. Then, as quickly as you slipped into that dream, woooosh, you are slung out of it back into the present day, amid bellows of 'Come on, mum!!! It's only a tenner, why are you being so stingy?' and you can't help but wishing they were little again – when you were the boss, not them.

If this is you, you will dream of bathing and feeding them as babies again, changing their nappies, reading bedtime stories and remembering how they looked at you as if you were the most important thing in the world to them. Because you were.

Now you are faced with them speaking back to you, sulking, lying and occasionally throwing tantrums at how 'unfair' you are being, despite how much you will protest it's 'for their own good'. Now you are merely a bank machine and someone reliable who will wash their knickers.

'Where did that cherubic, adorable and beautiful baby of mine go,' you think, as you drift off again, wondering that maybe when you wake up the next time the children will be five again, tugging on your skirt and asking for a piggy-back ride.

Always-bragging-to-the-neighbours Mum

Neighbours are strange beasts. Half friend, half enemy. They will feed the cat while you're on holiday, but also snoop through your stuff as they do so. Plus, neighbour-to-neighbour conversations rarely discuss anything other than each other's children – it's a swap shop of gossip and maternal pride.

Oh, and gloating, should you be this type of mum.

Always-bragging-to-the-neighbours mum will relish the

prospect of bumping into a neighbour at the local paper shop for a chance to update them (for hours on end sometimes) on how well their children are getting on in their first year at Oxford, how many A+'s they got in the summer exams or how they are currently travelling to some exotic, far-away destination and will, no doubt, come back 'well rounded'.

Mums are proud creatures by nature, and while pride sometimes can get the better of them, talking about their children (who no longer live at home any more) closes up the painful distance between them.

Have you seen this Mum?

Other people always regret asking mums 'how are the kids?' as the answer tends to take forever and eat into their day and, before they know it, they haven't got half as much stuff done as they'd hoped.

Cuddle-hungry Mum

Mums love huggles – a combination of hugs and cuddles – and big kisses. While these are more difficult to squeeze out of older children, they are very enthusiastically received by young children and mums know this – squeezing them for all they are worth, every moment they can, no matter where they might be. Cue spontaneous cuddles in the middle of Sainsbury's, or a massive hug in the car park – mums will take whatever they can get, whenever they can get it.

It doesn't matter if the child is a toddler (and can't defend themselves) or at university, a cuddle-hungry mum will strike at any time, with a kiss and a long bear hug, and be totally oblivious of where she might be or how inappropriate (for the child) it may appear. She could be outside the school gates or congratulating her daughter on a 2:1, a cuddle-hungry mum doesn't mind – all that matters is a lingering hug that lasts for as long as the child lets her. Of course, the child will squirm, fight and wriggle out of the hug after not too long and the mum might squeeze just a little harder before letting go again. But one thing's for sure, it won't be long until mum is hungry again!

Loves-her-garden Mum

Gardens are havens for mums, especially once the children have grown up and left the family home, as mums are able to focus their attention, their unconditional love, on something else that will grow and blossom with the benefit of their TLC – now that the kids have vanished. A mum's love is never-ending and without the kids to fuss and fight over any more, the garden will receive it instead. And the garden won't moan about it either or talk back. A garden will feed on a mother's love and reciprocate it without asking for money or a lift to Carl's house. Gardens are a place where mums can flourish, be creative and have their own space.

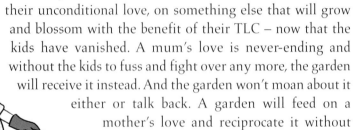

Rivalry between mum's and the neighbours' gardens are also well known. Not content with competing over whose child did better academically this year or whose husband has the biggest wine cellar (or smallest beer belly) a major maternal one-upmanship is usually fought out in the garden. Who has the better flowerbeds? Whose home-grown vegetables are the straightest? Whose sunflower grows the tallest? And are *their* bushes encroaching over *our* fence?

The garden is the place where mum can find solace and peace of mind, but she can also go to war with Sheila at number 52 if she wants!

Growing-old-disgracefully Mum

Some mums loathe the idea of growing old gracefully. They hate it. It sounds boring and after having spent the past twenty years or so looking after other people, they'll be absolutely confident that the last part of their lives is not spent throwing the towel in and forever watching *Coronation Street*.

After the kids have left home (only to return when they need their washing done) these mums like to experiment, take chances, live life again – just as they did before they became burdened by children. They like to roam free, meet friends and act like teenagers themselves again! And why not! Their lives are theirs again, so why grow old gracefully when there is a whole new world out there to explore.

So instead of buying knitting needles and wool and settling down with a cup of tea in front of the telly, this type of mum is out the door, booking holidays with friends, enjoying life and doing all the things that she's always wanted to do. Maybe a spot of bungee jumping? Or learning to scuba dive? Or salsa classes! Or maybe nothing quite as big as that, maybe she just wants to keep it simple. How about a tattoo? Just a little one and for dad's eyes only. Just a little symbol to show the world that she refuses to go down with the ship (i.e. her body), that there's still life in the old girl yet and that life doesn't end when the kids leave the roost. If anything, life begins again.

Embarrassing-dancer Mum

Yes, this means you. How do I know? Well, does this sound familiar? Two thumbs aloft, hips swaying out of time, head nodding in time, eyes closed, massive grin on your face as if you are caught in the very personal grasp of Mr Tom Jones. Is this you? Are you the embarrassing dancer always the first on the dance floor at family gatherings? Were you the one caught on camera, limbs flailing, your thumbs acting like hypnotic beacons for the rest of the family to watch and blush in shame, while dad grumbles to Uncle Tom that 'she's not with us I swear'.

The 'two thumbs aloft' dance move is often attributed to mums who have forgotten what to do with their hands when they dance. Where once as a younger gal you would have flailed them around wildy with reckless abandon, but now, now you're a mother, you gently lift your thumbs aloft and swing randomly, and unpredictably, in and out of time.

Don't worry, it's not as if you are the only mum dancing this way, all mums – over a certain age, lets say 38 – dance this way. A whole dance floor of embarrassing-dancer mums, thumbs stuck in the air, is a truly awe-inspiring sight…of course, nowhere near as funny as all the dads circling around the outside of the dance floor, beer in hand, pretending they are way too cool!

Famous Mums Through the Ages: A Timeline!

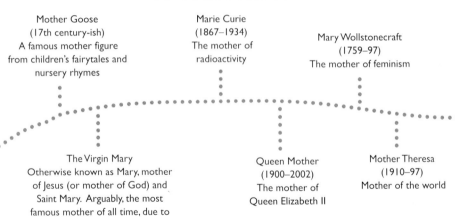

Mother Goose
(17th century-ish)
A famous mother figure
from children's fairytales and
nursery rhymes

Marie Curie
(1867–1934)
The mother of
radioactivity

Mary Wollstonecraft
(1759–97)
The mother of feminism

The Virgin Mary
Otherwise known as Mary, mother
of Jesus (or mother of God) and
Saint Mary. Arguably, the most
famous mother of all time, due to
her Immaculate Conception

Queen Mother
(1900–2002)
The mother of
Queen Elizabeth II

Mother Theresa
(1910–97)
Mother of the world

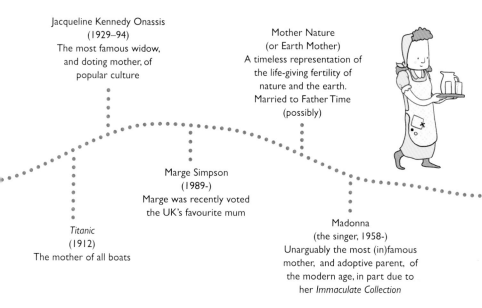

Jacqueline Kennedy Onassis
(1929–94)
The most famous widow,
and doting mother, of
popular culture

Mother Nature
(or Earth Mother)
A timeless representation of
the life-giving fertility of
nature and the earth.
Married to Father Time
(possibly)

Marge Simpson
(1989-)
Marge was recently voted
the UK's favourite mum

Titanic
(1912)
The mother of all boats

Madonna
(the singer, 1958-)
Unarguably the most (in)famous
mother, and adoptive parent, of
the modern age, in part due to
her *Immaculate Collection*

The SuperMum

This is one of the most common mums you see flying around local supermarkets, schools, high streets and swimming pools every day. Forget Superman! SuperMum is much more impressive! Plus she can multi-task which, because Superman is a man, he can't. Supermum can defeat multiple bad stains, school bullies, body odours and bowls of Bran Flakes in one clean sweep without breaking into a sweat. Even if she has three hungry kids underneath her feet, a car full of shopping, a busy day at work, a house full of chores, a stressed-out husband and a daughter poorly with a cold, it doesn't matter, SuperMum never disappoints anyone with her super abilities to be ten places at once. Not only does she have ultrasonic hearing ('the twins are fighting upstairs again!') she can also shatter windows just by shouting really loud and she can also clean, cook *and* care in one laser-guided, lightning-quick move. All in time for *Eastenders* on the sofa with a cup of tea and a biscuit and a cuddle with dad. And if by the time she goes to bed everyone in the house is safe, content and happy then SuperMum has saved the day again.

Have you seen this Mum?

A SuperMum has all the powers of a superhero and sometimes wears her knickers on the outside of her clothes too – but that's only because she was in a rush that morning!

House-proud Mum

Some mums love nothing more than to run around picking up after their children – they love scrubbing the toilet again two minutes after having just spent ten minutes cleaning the same toilet. Mums love trying to remove mud that has been ground into their new carpet and they can't wait for the next time a whole pint of Ribena is spilt all down the living room wall. It's what a house-proud mum lives for. She dreams of it.

Really?
No, of course not.

Even the most obsessive or house-proud mum doesn't want to spend every moment of her day cleaning, and then recleaning, the house if she doesn't have to.

But that doesn't mean that a house-proud mum doesn't enjoy pampering the family home, getting a thrill out of making the place clean, tidy and spotless for when the kids, and dad, come home from school and work. And even if it only stays clean and spotless for 5 minutes, and even if no one notices or gives her any credit, a house-proud mum won't mind because she has proof that she worked hard – a sore back, worn-out fingers, tired legs and aching arms. Why do you think mums like facials, manicures, back and foot rubs so much? It's because they're the parts of the body that need the attention after all that scrubbing!

More-dad-than-dad Mum

When it comes to running a family home, dads, let's be honest, are utterly rubbish. For all emergencies and domestic issues, the kids always run straight to mum. They know that dad would just send them to mum anyway, not because he's cruel, but because he's lazy or incompetent.

In many households, mum and dad split the responsibilities. In some houses dad does the manly jobs (e.g. taxi-ing and burying dead pets) and mum does the more responsible stuff such as being the chef and chief organiser of everyone. In my house, mum was both. If anything needed doing, you'd go straight to

mum – she'd know where the bandages were kept, where the bike pumps were, she knew how to fix the plumbing and how to get the shower as hot as the sun. She even knew how to use the various combinations of remote controls used to power a collection of differing TVs, stereos and tape recorders (which is more than dad ever could).

Have you seen this Mum?

More-dad-than-dad mums can be seen in the garage fixing bikes and dimmer switches and painting the downstairs loo and building flat pack furniture while dad is out on the golf course.

Keep-fit-at-the-gym Mum

The gym is a fairly new place for mums to hang out – they used to stay away from where young people like to go and sweat. However, when they realised that all that birthday cake was still hanging around a month after their birthday – mainly  around their hips – mums of all ages descended upon gyms in their droves. Whether it was to enjoy aqua classes, spinning, dance classes, swimming or even hardcore cardio sessions with a personal trainer named Thor, mums who had once enjoyed the cravings of pregnancy , or used to enjoy finishing off the kids' leftovers, were now sick of being cuddly. They now want a body just like that woman off telly, you know, her off *Strictly Come Dancing*.

Have you seen this Mum?

A keep-fit-at-the-gym mum can resist all temptation! Even when dad is scoffing on Dairy Milk, this type of mum has the strength of a thousand bears to resist even one little square of wholenut by rationing that, for every square of chocolate she eats, that's another two miles at the gym she needs to run!

Turning-into-her-own-mum Mum

There comes a time in every mum's life when she has to accept a few inevitable facts.

One, no matter how much anti-wrinkle cream you slop all over your skin, the wrinkles will keep coming. You can try to fight it, but nature, evolution and genetics will always win.

Two, the children – no matter how much they scream 'I'll never leave you, mummy' when they are seven years old – they will leave you the very second they turn eighteen. This is hard for any mother to accept. Unfortunately, kids can't stay kids forever no matter how much you wish it to be true.

And finally, all mums over the course of their own lifetimes will turn into their own mother.

Now, this can either be a good or bad thing depending on your point of view. Many mums will recoil in horror at the thought of turning into their mother, noting all her flaws as she has grown older and desperately hoping not to inherit her lines. However, some will obviously love the idea of turning into the woman who raised them so well and who was always there for them and was the best mother in the world. Which one are you?

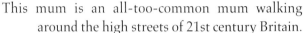

Embraces-the-21st-Century Mum

This mum is an all-too-common mum walking around the high streets of 21st century Britain. This is the type of mum who sees her children desperately yearning for iPods, iPhones, mobiles, Apple Macs, mp3s, laptops, internet, Skype, email, Facebook, MySpace, Bebo, Flickr and wants a piece of the action! If it means being able to interact with their children digitally – and bring them closer, rather than being left behind – then this type of mum wants in, and is aching to be seen as cool!

Even though you have to squint at the screen or think the buttons are too small or don't understand half the things your new iPhone 3G does (it's a phone, you think) you embrace the technological revolution because you understand and appreciate that it is designed to bring people together, to share, to interact, to be part of each other's lives even if you are distances apart.

Scared-of-the-21st-century Mum

Some mums think that technology is for young people and that they are 'too old to learn' how to use new technologies such as mp3 players, the internet or mobile phones. These are the type of mums who still listen to cassette tapes, FM radio and get letterheaded paper with their address on. Nothing wrong with that, of course.

A scared-of-the-21st-century mum wishes things were simple, back to the 'olden' days when people used to write letters to one another, pop round each other's houses for cups of tea and talk face to face and communicate via the old-fashioned ways rather than all these impersonal fancy gizmos and gadgets that half the time don't work and cost an arm, a leg and a few toes.

A scared-of-the-21st century mum doesn't feel the need to be seen as 'cool' by her children and doesn't mind trips to the library to find something out rather than using Google. Despite her protestations that she doesn't need it, her husband bought her a mobile phone and so she is forever peering over her reading glasses wondering why the 'screen is so bloody small!' and constantly asking why people keep sending her messages that end with :) LOL!

Circles-TV-programmes-with-a highlighter-in-the-Radio Times Mum

Ready, Steady, Cook is on (the greens are winning, as usual) so now is the perfect time for this type of mum to highlight all the TV programmes for the forthcoming seven days that she wants to watch. It's a greatly rewarding task and she finds comfort in the excitement of knowing that her next week's telly schedule is organised no matter what happens.

Some days this mum will highlight programmes recklessly with wild abandon, throwing caution to the wind, some days she'll restrain yourself and hold back, come to her senses, and realise that *Casualty* had its chance and is no longer a highlight-able inevitability.

You'll highlight daily programmes like *The One Show* even though they are on every day at the same time, just for consistency and neatness. You'll even highlight programmes that dad may be interested in. Though he won't take any notice.

Have you seen this Mum?

While the kids are busy recording all their programmes on Sky+, whizzing through the interactive TV service, you can't be bothered with all that nonsense and prefer the old-fashioned way. And besides, you rather enjoy the peace and quiet of sitting down and circling your programmes with a cup of tea.

Keeps-secrets-from-dad Mum

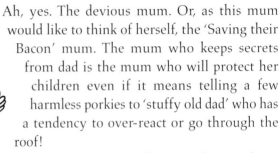

Ah, yes. The devious mum. Or, as this mum would like to think of herself, the 'Saving their Bacon' mum. The mum who keeps secrets from dad is the mum who will protect her children even if it means telling a few harmless porkies to 'stuffy old dad' who has a tendency to over-react or go through the roof!

A good example of this is when, perhaps, after the teenage daughter recently backed the car into a lamppost. Knowing how dad would react (take away the keys!), mum stepped in like the hero she is and took the blame (or most probably, blamed the neighbour).

Mums are always taking the blame for their kids, or lending them money, even though they know it's behind dad's back and he would be a bit miffed if he found out his authority was being undermined. Dad likes to play bad cop because he knows mum lets kids get away with murder and will always play the good cop. When it comes to cover-ups the mum who keeps secrets from dad is a legend, always claiming, with a smile on her face, that 'maybe it was the cat' who spilled sticky cola down his favourite, reclining leather chair.

New-age-spiritual Mum

Otherwise known as 'hippy mum', a new age mum is a mum very much with her head in the clouds, very chilled, relaxed, living a bohemian, carefree lifestyle. Nowadays a hippy mum, sorry, new-age mum, practices yoga, meditates, has a macrobiotic diet and a health food shop loyalty card and very rarely has anything to do with the real world or 'The Man'. This type of mum probably doesn't own a TV or a mobile phone, claiming she 'doesn't trust them', and will no doubt use tarot cards to determine whether or not today will be the day that she decides to buy a lottery ticket.

A new-age mum may have not always been this way so her children will no doubt be grounded and live in the real world and always trying to persuade her to buy a mobile phone so that they can get hold of her and tell her to stop worrying about government conspiracies – she may well be right, but not owning a credit card isn't going to stop them. A new-age mum is completely loveable if sometimes a bit bonkers, but then aren't all mums?

Falls-asleep-five-minutes-into-the-film Mum

As far as I am aware, all mums fall asleep within five minutes into the film or TV programme they are watching. And who can blame them?

After a busy day cooking, cleaning, sweeping, wiping, bathing and tucking in – a mum must surely be all tuckered out! The very minute she gets any free time to herself to sit down in front of the TV and catch up on her recorded programmes, the very minute her bum hits the sofa, and the lights go out, mum's off – drooling and gently snoring – all the while still wearing her apron.

Dads will sometimes try and encourage mum to sit through a whole movie that he's rented without her falling asleep, but it never works – a busy mum has zonked out not long after the opening credits only to wake up halfway through and ask 'What's happening? Who's he? And why did she do that?' much to the groans of everyone. Dad just sits there and laughs and tries to condense the whole plot into a few lines – only for mum to fall asleep again five minutes later.

Have you seen this Mum?

Only if it's a Brad Pitt film or a rom-com with Hugh Grant, will a fall-asleep-five minutes-into-the-film mum stay wide awake, glued to the sappy plot, until dad starts complaining that the movie makes no sense and mum has to repeatedly shush him to be quiet.

Baby-photos-always-at-the -ready Mum

Usually kept by the front door for ultra-quick convenience when your teenage son walks through the door with his new girlfriend or (if you are a particularly devilish mum) a group of male friends before his 18th birthday party!

This embarrassing baby nostalgia – full of the historical riches that every child dreads – is designed to playfully strike fear, panic and devastation into your children's lives. What fun!

Being the type of mum you are you leave no shame undiscovered, no embarrassing photo album page unturned, and you are relentless in your quest to find the most toe-curling picture of all time. Favourite photographs will undoubtedly include the paddling pool shot of 1983 when your son's willy is on show or when your daughter first learned to use a potty and was caught with her pants around her ankles smiling as if she had achieved Olympic Gold. New boyfriends and girlfriends love this and usually bleat 'awwwww!' so it's not all bad, you suppose.

However, you know that you are blinded by unconditional pride and the motherly belief that 'The kids love it really', when, of course, the absolute opposite is true.

Constantly Baking Mum

Nothing makes a child run home from school faster than knowing there is a delicious pie, cake or hot home-made meal waiting on the table for them, especially after a drizzly netball practice or unfair class detention. It's the first lesson any mother learns – and any mum that keeps a happy home knows that the way to their children's hearts is through their constantly rumbling tummies.

Home-made baking makes heroes out of mums – especially Rice Krispie cakes and a cup of tea at just the right time – it turns normally wild, unruly kids into angelic disciples. Home-cooked baking also acts perfectly as a bridging 'I'm sorry' if they catch you going through their text messages and the first day of school doesn't seem so hard when they come home and are offered a fresh-out-of-the-oven cookie and a big hug.

Waits-up-until-they're-home Mum

Waiting up for your teenage child to come home late after a night out is one of the most mischievous acts a mother can do. Especially when they pretend that they are just 'catching up with the ironing'. At 1am.

Mums wait up for these precious ten minutes when their grown-up 'babies' walk through the door, always slightly 'tired and emotional' and when they are at their weakest, most vulnerable and, most importantly, at their most verbal – a merry teenager is intoxicated enough to spill the beans on what's really happening in their lives (as opposed to the PG friendly version they tell you when sober!). In those valuable moments mums can find out where their children go at night, who with, what normally happens and whether that boy from next door can really be trusted?

This information becomes priceless for the times when your grown-up child fails to arrive home at the promised time – it means you know where they are likely to be and makes your storming there in rage a whole lot easier!

For a few precious hours the next morning the mum who waits up not only knows everything, but has enough dirt to keep their embarrassed kids nicely behaved until teatime.

One-glass-of-Pinot-Grigio and-she's-tipsy Mum

Since the birth of your first child, alcohol has been reserved to a glass of wine (with dinner) every birthday or occasionally when friends come round and force you into 'letting your hair down'.

You decided to give up all alcohol for fear you may one day receive a phone call at 11pm from your teenage child who has somehow become lost in a dark wood and needs someone to pick them up. The likelihood of this happening is slim,

but you rationalise that 'you never know' is a good excuse. And seeing as your husband is normally in no fit state to drive after 8pm, that someone is always you anyway.

If you do drink, one glass of white wine (usually Pinot Grigio, I bet) is all it takes for you to be swinging from the rafters, fumbling your words, speaking in flirty innuendo that makes no sense to man nor beast and giggling uncontrollably. After a glass of champagne on New Year's Eve you've become the life and soul of the party – but, as predicted by dad, you will be found slumped on the sofa snoring by 11.55pm.

Have you seen this Mum?

This type of mum likes to remain in control most of the time but when she does let her hair down she goes crazy and has a good time, usually making dad have to apologise that 'she doesn't drink that often' as mum stands leaning against the wall talking to the hat-stand.